transparencies

Mission Theological Advisory Group

transparencies

pictures of mission through prayer and reflection –
an accompaniment to *Presence and Prophecy*

edited by Anne Richards

CHURCH HOUSE
PUBLISHING

Church House Publishing
Church House
Great Smith Street
London SW1P 3NZ

Churches Together in Britain
and Ireland
Inter-Church House
35–41 Lower Marsh
London SE1 7SA

ISBN 0 7151 5550 4

GS Misc 690

Typeset in Franklin Gothic 9pt

Printed by The Cromwell Press Ltd,
Trowbridge, Wiltshire

Published 2002 for the Board of
Mission of the Archbishops' Council
by Church House Publishing and
Churches Together in Britain
and Ireland.

contents

members of the Mission Theological Advisory Group 1996–2001

The Mission Theological Advisory Group is set up jointly by the Archbishops' Council's Board of Mission within the Church of England and the Churches' Commission on Mission of Churches Together in Britain and Ireland. It includes members from the Church of England, Roman Catholic, Methodist, Church of Scotland, Church in Wales and Congregationalist traditions.

chairman

The Rt Revd Dr Michael Nazir-Ali

members

The Revd Dr Martyn Atkins (to 1998)
The Revd Dr Brian Castle
The Rt Revd Richard Garrard
The Revd Canon Dr Graham Kings
Dr Alwyn Marriage (from 1999)
The Revd Joanna Penberthy
The Rt Revd Peter Price
The Revd Fr Frank Regan
The Revd Alison White (to 1998)
The Revd Dr Chris Wigglesworth
The Revd Dr Andrew Wood (from 1999)
The Revd Dr Janet Wootton

staff

Mr Simon Barrow (from 2000)
Mr John Clark (from 2000)
The Revd Donald Elliott (to 2000)
The Revd Canon Philip King (to 2000)
Dr Anne Richards (secretary)

preface

In the introduction to his book of Biblical meditations, *Jesus, Lamb of God*, written in 1996,[1] Bishop David Atkinson talks about the excitement of shining a light through painted glass plates to project a picture on to a white wall. He and his brother went further, shining the light through several glass plates to create a composite picture, making a whole new image from several different parts. In this way, he recalls something that has been characteristic of the material in this book – there is an excitement and a joy in theological reflection, because the experience of thinking, praying, meditating and sharing can lead us into new places we have not anticipated. Prayer and reflection can bring forgotten memories to the surface, tap into deep emotions, create different paths of reasoning and, above all, surprise and delight us by uncovering new ways for us to find what God is doing here among us.

Yet theological reflection in the context of prayer and fellowship is not merely an internal, self-pleasing exercise, for it unfolds for us questions about what our life should be in the service of mission. This book, therefore, sets out some ways of engaging in theological reflection, but the images and ideas that may materialize are not ends in themselves – like pictures for a photograph album – but, rather, signposts for a larger journey. That journey is the one to which all of us are called, a journey on which we seek continually to discern the will of God, to make Jesus Christ known and to show to others the creative, illuminating Spirit forever at work in the world.

The Rt Revd Dr Michael Nazir-Ali
Bishop of Rochester
Chair of the Mission Theological Advisory Group

acknowledgements

I am grateful to all my friends in the Mission Theological Advisory Group and especially to Janet Wootton and Graham Kings for their help and kindness in making the presentations available for publication in this form.

I am also grateful to Joanna Cox and to Janice Price for their advice about the application of this material to group work.

I am especially grateful to Graham Kings for allowing me to include a number of his poems, which he shared with the group but has published elsewhere, principally in *Guidelines*, Bible Reading Fellowship, September–December 2000.

Anne Richards

copyright acknowledgements

introduction

When the Mission Theological Advisory Group began a new project in 1997, we found ourselves thrown together as 'professional' people given a job to do by meeting four times a year for the matter of a few hours. Coming from different churches and from different parts of the British Isles, we all had to commit time and energy to the journey to come together in London. Typically, a group such as ours would work to a tight agenda of business in order to get as much done as possible in the time allowed. Work would begin with a short prayer commending the meeting to God and would close with the grace.

It soon became clear, however, that this 'business' style of doing theology and resourcing the churches was not enough. While it was what we were used to, with 'minutes' and 'matters arising' and all the rest, we had questions about how we could do theology together, how our creativity could be released and how we could share and explore as friends, not just as ecumenical partners with a job to do.

So we decided that we would devote a significant period at each meeting to a time of prayer and reflection, which would be unrelated to the agenda. One of us would prepare a theological reflection that would be the spark for conversation, sharing and prayer about our faith, doubts, hopes, fears and dreams. This sharing would take place in a safe space in which we could talk freely about our thoughts and trust each other to respect and to respond to each other's ideas and feelings, even when we disagreed. We spent time in prayer, we sang hymns. We laughed, we were sombre, we offered personal experiences and insights. Sometimes we just sat in silence. And, although all this took time out of the business, we found that doing the job we had been assigned became energized by our reflection, engagement, theological exploration, and discernment of the amazing diversity and creative energy of God's Holy Spirit.

This book seeks to take the material from some of those times of reflection and sets them out as the heart of a resource for others. The chapters are based on the material we used in the group, but they are not intended to be prescriptive, the last word on the subject. Each can be taken and used in different ways by different individuals or groups. We offer some of our conversation and ideas, but there are many other conversations and ideas to be enjoyed. In addition, we offer suggestions for discussion, prayers, hymns, meditations and Bible study. The design and construction of each chapter is entirely open and can be dismantled and reassembled differently according to time, place and the people using it. All the materials are offered as a stimulus to creative exploration and to encourage everyone to reflect theologically on mission. But this is also a book that does not have to be read strictly in order and can be dipped into at any of the different chapters.

We have given this book the title *Transparencies* firstly, because each theological reflection is like a photographic transparency waiting for illumination to make the picture sharper, clearer, more brightly coloured; secondly, because we have learned that theological reflection provides a window that we may gaze upon, but also look through, into the extraordinary beauty of God's kingdom. Part of the delight of being not just a group, but a family, is that we have discovered that things as diverse as the Holy Bible and the Bluewater shopping centre, the Harry Potter books and Isaac Watts' great hymns can offer us new insights into God's ways with the world.

Transparencies may also be used in association with the *Presence and Prophecy Study Guide* by Simon Barrow, Church House Publishing/Church Together in Britain and Ireland, 2002.

some ways of using this material

Each of the chapters in this book sets out material for theological reflection on a particular broad-based topic. The intention is that an initial image or theme becomes the focus of a reflection that can open out in any number of different ways. How we use this 'transparency' to reveal an image entirely depends on our own responses. The intention, however, is that wherever the initial image or theme leads us, it can help us think about our own vocation to serve God, the way in which we follow Christ and the way we can make Christ known in the world. This is at the heart of our task in mission. There are no 'right' answers, but we hope that each exploration helps us to think, pray and reflect more deeply on what the Holy Spirit is prompting us to do.

Individual readers using this book may wish to use the theological reflection and thoughts from the group as a way of joining with us in the long conversation that has been at the heart of our work together. The other sections of the chapter therefore become peripheral support for the central in-depth engagement with aspects of the popular culture that surrounds us. Individual readers may further wish to read the whole work from which extracts are taken, or explore the further resources suggested.

Groups may wish to use the theological reflection material only as background for a time together that focuses more on the initial image or theme, using the prayer, music and Bible study as a way of allowing the group to draw out and engage with the ideas more effectively. We have not sought to be prescriptive about the way in which different groups may wish to do this, and the material may be adapted to different models of group work.

There is further material available to adapt the chapters to particular interests or needs. For example, if groups are especially interested in the Harry Potter debate in working with children, or supporting people with terminal illness, or suffering from abuse, there are other resources that have come to us during the work of the group. Contact Dr Anne Richards, Church House, Great Smith Street, London SW1P 3NZ.

vision

Rublev's icon.

We used Douglas Coupland's novel *Girlfriend in a Coma* to consider the message of an unusual 'angel' and the vision of an opportunity to change both our own lives and our world.

prayer

Eternal God,
you sent your angels into our world.
They brought Good News, they brought challenge,
they offered hope to unlikely people.
Send your angel to us, open our hearts
to your presence in the world.
Amen.

theological reflection

Douglas Coupland, *Girlfriend in a Coma*[1]

This book is opened and closed by an angel, Jared,[2] who died as a teenager of leukaemia. He introduces us at the beginning of this novel to the end of the world:

Yes, the world is over. It's still *here*, but it's . . . *over*. I'm at the End of the World. Dust in the wind. The end of the world as we know it. Just another brick in the wall. It sounds glamorous but it's not. It's dreary and quiet and the air always smells like there's a tire fire half a mile up wind.

Let me describe the real estate that remains one year after the world ended: It is above all a silent place with no engines or voices or music. Theater screens fray and unravel like overworn shirts. Endless cars and trucks and minivans sit on road shoulders harboring cargoes of rotted skeletons behind the wheel. Homes across the world collapse and fall inward on themselves; pianos, couches and microwaves tumble through floors and expose money and love notes hidden within the floorboards. Most foods and medicines have time-expired. The outer world is eroded by rain, and confused by lightning. Fires still burn, of course, and the weather now tends to extremes.

Suburban streets such as those where I grew up are dissolving inside rangy and shaggy overgrown plants; vines unfurl across roads now undriven by Camaros. Tennis rackets silently unstring inside dark dry closets. Ten million pictures fall from ten million walls. Road signs blister and rust. Hungry dogs roam in packs.

To visit earth now you would see thousands of years of grandeur and machinery all falling asleep. Cathedrals fall as readily as banks; car assembly lines as readily as supermarkets. Lightless sunken submarines lumber to the ocean's bottom to spend the next billion years collecting silt. In cities the snow sits unplowed; jukeboxes sit silent; chalkboards stand forever unerased. Computer databases lie untapped while power cables float from aluminum towers like long, thin hairs. (pp. 4–5)

In the central part of this story are six people: Karen, Richard, Pam, Hamilton, Wendy and Linus. We meet them as teenagers being swept along by the culture. Karen is starving herself to death trying to get into a size five swimsuit. Pam and Hamilton are taking cocaine. Wendy and Linus are immersed in science and technology. They are 'netheads' and video watchers.

Karen has a dark vision of the end of the world and writes it down as a prophecy, a warning. *God is watching*. Shortly afterwards she falls into a coma and into a persistent vegetative state. Is she alive or dead? And what does her unconsciousness have to do with her visions? While in this state she gives birth to a girl, but what does this new birth mean in the face of her vision of the end of the world? Richard, her boyfriend, becomes indecisive and alcoholic, unable to make up his mind about being a father to Megan, his daughter. Pam and Ham become serious heroin addicts after Pam's supermodel status wears off. They end up working for the plastic and facile aspects of the movie industry, creating special effects for monster movies. Linus and Wendy marry without love and deal with this by overworking and becoming vacant and uncommunicative.

Then Karen wakes up. Her friends have to deal with a teenager in an aged and wasted body. What does it mean to be young and fresh and have all your life before you in your head when your body in which you live is broken and lost to you? What does 'too late' mean for somebody like Karen? Further, how does this compare to what the drug addicts have done to their bodies, and to what Linus has done to *his* mind? One thing is certain: Karen's coma had purpose. But what was it *for*?

Jared the angel comes to tell them the answer. Karen's ability to see the present through the eyes of the past person she was and is now, is testimony or testament, to enlighten her friends and to make them wake up. Her perception is different, for heaven is very close, but we who live now have forgotten about making it our ambition.

> Every single second of our lives we're crossing a finish line of some sort, with heaven's roaring cheers surrounding us as we win our way forward. Our smallest acts – crossing a street, peeling an apple . . . are as though we are ripping an Olympic ribbon to thunderous applause. The universe *wants* us to win. (p. 232)

The friends have chosen to witness the end of the world. All around them other human beings fall asleep and die and then rot. How do they react? Typically,

> . . . useless sacks of dung *they* are, slumped around Karen's fireplace watching an endless string of videos, the floor clogged with Kleenex boxes and margarine tubs overflowing with diamonds and emeralds, rings and gold bullion – a parody of wealth. (p. 209)

As Jared goes to each one he assesses what this experience means to them in terms of what they could have done with their lives. For example, Linus:

'Jared, I *know* that God can come at any moment in any form. I *know* we always have to be on the alert. And I *know* that day and night are the same to God. And I *know* that God never changes. But all I ever wanted was just a *clue.*' (pp. 235–6) 'All this time and all this exposure to every conceivable aspect of life – wisdom so rarely enters the picture. We barely have enough time to figure out who we are and then we become bitter and isolated as we age.' (p.237)

Linus is rewarded with a glimpse of heaven.

Jared heals his friends. He brings about Wendy's pregnancy; he restores Karen's wasted legs; he cleans the drug addicts' minds and bodies, so that they feel truly washed and sinless; he repairs a brain-damaged baby. With these gifts, they are all also given a second chance, to go back to the moment when Karen woke up, except this time Karen will not wake and they are left to go on with their new understanding: to live with the knowledge of the end of the world.

Jared puts into effect what he calls 'Plan B':

'And in your new lives you'll have to live entirely for that one sensation – that of imminent truth. And you're going to have to holler for it, steal for it, beg for it . . .' (p. 268) 'Every day for the rest of your lives, all of your living moments are to be spent making others aware of this need – the need to probe and drill and examine and locate the words that take us to beyond ourselves.

Scrape. Feel. Dig. Believe. *Ask.*' (p. 269)

The novel ends with this important affirmation:

You'll soon be seeing us walking down your street, our backs held proud, our eyes dilated with truth and power. We might look like you, but you should know better. We'll draw our line in the sand and force the world to cross our line. Every cell in our body explodes with the truth. We *will* be kneeling in front of the Safeway, atop out-of-date textbooks whose pages we have chewed out. We'll be begging passers by to see the need to question and question and question and never stop questioning until the world stops spinning. We'll be adults who smash the tired, exhausted system. We'll crawl and chew and dig our way into a radical new world. We will change minds and souls from stone and plastic into linen and gold – that's what I believe. That's what I know. (p. 281)

some thoughts from the group

When we think about what it means to be the Church in mission we often confine ourselves to imagining the here and now. We want to reach out, to share our faith with others *right now*. If we have a plan, a vision, it can be very short-term and localized. Yet in Matthew 28.19, the Great Commission, Jesus says: 'Go therefore and make disciples of all nations, baptizing them in the name of the Father and of the Son and of the Holy Spirit, and teaching them to obey everything that I have commanded you. And remember, I am with you always, to the end of the age.' The context for our mission is Jesus' promise to be with us until the end of time, but how often do we think about God's final purpose for the whole creation and what our part in it might be?

We found the end of the novel inspiring because it speaks of powerful transformation from the mundane to the rare and the precious. The vision of the end of the world in this book is very powerful, especially when we consider how scenes of desolation, war and destruction invade our living rooms through today's technology. What impact do these images have on us? However, although there is a danger in the materialism of our society, we should not forget there is a capricious spirituality also at work. Coupland reminds us to be aware that the Church is not always attractive to young people but that the power of God is still evident, even in the underside of our materialistic society. Would we recognize Jared as a messenger of God? Are we too comfortable with our own lives to go to the smashed-up world of the mentally ill, the drug addicts, the marginalized and forgotten people and to find God at work among them? Are Christians asked to work to Plan B, when the world is hell-bent on Plan A? How can we do this in our own situation?

poem: Jesus goes underground

She listens to her Walkman
       living in another world,
       ignoring her neighbour as herself.
He reads The *Sun*
       immersed in actors' lives
       washing his mind with soap.
They do not touch,
       insulated, isolated;
       marriage withdrawal symptoms.
She scrunches monster munches,
       monosodium glutamate;
       bags of tasty emptiness.
He's stuck in sniffing glue,

> addicted to cheap death;
> nobody knows the trouble he's in.
>
> To bring them to their senses and together,
> Jesus goes Underground.
>
> He grabs the tube of glue
>   and breathes the breath of God.
> He throws the packet away
>   and gives her bread.
> He joins her hands in his
>   and brings them warmth.
> He folds the sun in half
>   and beams a smile.
> He slips the headphones from her ears
>   and shares his news.
>
> *Graham Kings*

other pathways for exploration

illustration, image or focus of meditation

We have chosen Rublev's icon of Abraham entertaining the angels unaware, but we find images of angels on many other pictures, posters and cards. Why do so many people believe in angels?

a purpose and a challenge

To ask ourselves what God's angel might be saying to us now. We have received the Good News – are we *really* willing to share it?

some wider discussion questions

● As Christians in mission, how can we bring about transformation in our local situation?

● How does the world around us appear to us?
   How is the world represented in newspapers, magazines, advertisements and in other media?

● How do we imagine God sees our world and what is happening to it?
   What does it mean for us to say, 'Christ will come again'?

● Do we think about the end of the world, the purpose and
meaning of our lives?
What events and experiences have changed our view of the world?

some suggested passages for Bible study

Numbers 22.31 ff
Luke 1.26-38
Revelation 21.1-8

meditation or music

Give me thy counsel for my guide
And then receive me to thy bliss:
All my desires and hopes beside
Are faint and cold, compared with this.

Isaac Watts, 'God of the morning, at whose voice . . .'[3]

some thoughts about mission

Are we on the alert for what God is saying to us? Who are God's
messengers today and do we entertain them unaware? Are we able
to say we have shared the Good News in the context in which we live
or is giving a second chance to people somebody else's problem?
What is our vision for our world? Do we even have one?

further resources

Some other novels by Douglas Coupland: *Generation X* (St Martin's
Press, 1991); *Microserfs* (HarperCollins, 1995); *Life after God* (Pocket
Books NY, 1994); *All Families are Psychotic* (St Martin's Press, 2001).
Films: *Trainspotting*, directed by Danny Boyle, Miramax, 1996; *Human
Traffic*, directed by Justin Kerrigan, IrishScreen/Metrodome (UK)
Miramax (US), 1999; *City of Angels*, directed by Brad Silberling, Warner
Bros, 2000; *It's a Wonderful Life*, directed by Frank Capra, RKO, 1946.[4]
Music: Robbie Williams: 'Angels' (on the *Angels* album, 2001); 'Eternity'
(single, 2001).

chapter 2

sacrifice

Peter Sales,
Pheonix, metal
sculpture, 1999.

We used the Harry Potter novels to look again at the theme of sacrifice and its relation to mission.

prayer

God of Surprises,
you offer us a life beyond the ordinary,
you promise us the mystery of eternity.
For this you gave us your only Son
who gave his life in order that we might live.
We thank you for your love for us
and for the new life given in Jesus Christ.
Amen.

theological reflection

The *Harry Potter* novels by J. K. Rowling

We are introduced to Harry Potter in the first book (and film) of the series as one of the powerless and the voiceless. He is a child, bullied

and victimized. He is orphaned, poor. His cousin has all
the material things that Harry is not allowed: cousin Dudley gets
everything he wants – a TV and a new bike, a cine camera . . . while
Harry gets to stay in his cupboard under the stairs. In our sort of
world, the selfish, materially driven world we live in, Harry is entirely
unprivileged. Like so many in our own society, he is at the bottom
of the heap, ignored, enslaved.

But, Harry has a history and a destiny that is known by others in
another world. He is called to be among them. No matter how hard
his aunt and uncle try to prevent it, the call (in the form of the giant
Hagrid with a letter of invitation) *cannot* be kept out. Harry is taken
to a bare rock in the middle of the sea, but Hagrid (on a fabulous flying
motorbike) still finds him. Harry does not see how he can enter the
magic world, but finds that in the magic bank, he literally has a pile
of hidden treasure, which he did not know he had. By responding to
the invitation he discovers both his real self and inheritance and the
true impoverishment of the material world. One comment is that it is
amazing how Muggles (the people of the non-magic world) manage
to get by without knowing this amazing other world and how many
inventions they produce to get by without it.

This magic world is beyond our solid, seemingly impenetrable world.
It is located beyond a barrier between platforms nine and ten at King's
Cross station. It is on the other side of a wall in a London pub. This
is the true, rich reality. In here, Harry finds fellowship and community
in his school. He discovers that he has a past and a history and that he
is loved and favoured. He discovers that he exists because his parents
died defending him from evil and their love protects him against all. At
the heart of this history lie truth, love and, above all, powerful sacrifice:

> 'Sir, there are some other things I'd like to know, if you can tell
> me . . . things I want to know the truth about . . .'

> 'The truth.' Dumbledore sighed. 'It is a beautiful and terrible thing,
> and should therefore be treated with great caution . . .'

> 'But why couldn't Quirrell touch me?'

> 'Your mother died to save you. If there is one thing Voldemort
> cannot understand, it is love. He didn't realise that love as powerful
> as your mother's for you leaves its own mark. Not a scar, no visible
> sign . . . to have been loved so deeply, even though the person who
> loved us is gone, will give us some protection for ever. It is in your

very skin. Quirrell, full of hatred, greed and ambition, sharing his soul with Voldemort, could not touch you for this reason. It was agony to touch a person marked by something so good.'[1]

In the school of the magic life, Harry learns important lessons. In Defence against the Dark Arts, Harry faces up to monsters, demons and the sources of evil in his world. He is given tools to fight these enemies by his teachers. He learns to overcome fear, to be willing in his turn to sacrifice himself to save others. His faith in the love and power of the headmaster protects Harry when he is alone and apparently defeated. Harry learns how to set wrongs right and restore the world by use of his gifts, his friendships, his faith, loyalty and determination. He is helped by unlikely people, including one creature that must suffer torture to help him and whom, in the end, he must rescue. He has to make moral judgements about right behaviour and to care for others. He learns the value of reconciliation, peace making and forgiveness. He has to take on the embodiment of evil: Lord Voldemort. Through his lessons in the Care of Magical Creatures he learns to nurture the creation and to cherish it.

Actual interest in so-called 'white magic' is discouraged. Divination is shown to be nonsense and is beautifully satirized as a waste of time. Superstitious fears are made harmless – Harry passes the time of day with ghosts and discovers that omens and horoscopes are laughable nonsense. Rather, the second book, *Harry Potter and the Chamber of Secrets* points to the more insidious seductions of the power of evil. A young lonely girl pours out her troubles to a magic diary, which writes back to her sympathetically, but then starts preying on her resentments and grudges to use her to destructive ends. Each story is a parable in its own right, with many layers of meaning and moral force.

As the books progress, Harry grows more wise and learns from his experiences, and the reader progresses with him on his magical journey. It is also a faith journey as Harry learns the depth and extent of Albus Dumbledore's wisdom. Both adults and children can identify with Harry or with his friends Ron and Hermione. There are many opportunities for exploring the big questions through Harry's adventures as when Harry ventures deep down into the bowels of the school to face the deadly basilisk, or when he discovers the truth of the betrayal which led to his parents' sacrificing themselves for him.

The mission questions for us arising from the Harry Potter novels and films concern how we can use the popular interest in Harry's story to ask people to look again at the selfish material world and the presence within it of Christian values – truth, love and, supremely, self-giving and sacrifice. Is this just to be a magic world in a story book or can it point to a world *we* want to make a reality?

some thoughts from the group

How do the people we seek to serve in mission approach fundamental questions about good and evil? Do they subscribe to an either/or world of good and bad, or is it more complicated, in that appearances can be deceptive as in the Harry Potter stories? In modern culture generally, there seems to be an interest in witches and wizards (*Buffy, Angel, Charmed*)[2] and in the possibility of another world in which a drama of good and evil is played out. Is this because an interest in the supernatural moves away from a totally explicable universe, the kind of universe offered us by people such as Richard Dawkins?[3] If so, we should not seek to downplay the Christian story. This has implications for the way we speak about Jesus Christ in refuting the Dawkins' view that there is no such thing as transcendence. People, though, *are* trying to find it, in spite of the reductionists. There may have been demythologizing, but people do want a greater, more inclusive vision of the truth. People are powerfully attracted by the story of loving sacrifice, as we may witness in the power of the film *Gladiator.*[4]

We might also learn more of this by looking at the interest in science fiction adventures. *Star Trek*, for example, has an impressive following. Despite Gene Roddenberry's assertions that *Star Trek* was intended to reflect no personal belief, the *Star Trek* films present a familiar paradigm: Spock sacrifices his life for others, 'the needs of the many outweigh the needs of the one . . . I have been and always shall be your friend'[5] and subsequently his immortal soul is returned to his regenerated body. Robed in white, he returns to his friends.

As Christians in mission we can forget the place of the transcendental and the supernatural in scripture. If we do this, we may end up offering people life without mystery. Yet in literature and in the media there are ways of thinking about the supernatural that are authentic. If we acknowledge this, then we too have an obligation to tell people about Jesus Christ as the one who is risen from the dead. But does the Church find it difficult to cope with the transcendental? Have we backed off from the real struggle and allowed the Church to become a tame, ghettoized chaplaincy to Western culture?

poem: turning point

Stalking in the garden in the heat of the moment
Reflecting on complexity of voluntary movement,
Slunk in listless and leaden despair,
Tangled, contorted and tearing his hair,
Rapping his head and wrapping his knees,
Rabidly ravaging under the trees,
Wanting to wait and waiting to want,
Weighing the longing of laying and font,
Augustine hears the Word of the Lord
Drifting, insisting the voice of a child:
'Tolle, lege: take it and read.
Tolle, lege: take it and read.'
Vocative discourse spoken by God,
Evocative sing-song challenge of a child.

Turning and turning he opens to read
The Word of the Lord in the words of St Paul:
'Lust and debauchery, revelry, rivalry,
Now is the time to wake from your sleep.'
Eloquent professor professes his call.

Now, no procrastination, delay;
Later is now, tomorrow today.

Graham Kings

other pathways for explorations

illustration, image or focus of meditation

A 'Harry Potter' image, or other image of fairytale or fantasy. Or play
an excerpt from the Harry Potter film, or other suitable fantasy film.

a purpose and a challenge

To remind ourselves of the depth of God's love for us and of the
sacrifice of Jesus Christ. But do we show people the power of sacrificial
love – and have we forgotten the power of wonder, mystery and awe in
our lives?

some wider questions for discussion

● As Christians in mission, how do we show others what God's
  kingdom is like?

How do we help people acquire the hope of heaven?

● How far does our society simply invent things to believe in?
What examples could we give of a 'pick'n'mix' spirituality?

● What does the idea that Jesus sacrificed his life for *all* people
really mean to us?
What would we be prepared to die for?

suggested passages for Bible study

Isaiah 53.1-10
Luke 24.36-53
1 Corinthians 13

meditation or music

Forbid it Lord, that I should boast
Save in the Cross of Christ my God;
All the vain things that charm me most,
I sacrifice them to his Blood.
Isaac Watts, 'When I survey the wondrous Cross'[6]

some thoughts about mission

What is it that so fascinates children and adults about the world of
Harry Potter? What longings and emotions are caught up in Harry's
story and in other fantasy stories? How does *our* story, the story of
Jesus, speak to the hopes, fears and dreams we encounter in other
people? How do we share with people a sense of the awe and majesty
of the eternal God?

further resources

The 'Culture' novels of Iain Banks.
The *Discworld* series of Terry Pratchett.
The *Star Wars* and *Star Trek* films and *Gladiator.*
C. S. Lewis, the *Narnia* series.
J. R. R. Tolkien, *The Lord of the Rings.*
Philip Pullman, *His Dark Materials* trilogy.

chapter 3
praise

We used (and sang) one of Isaac Watts' hymns to help us
look again at the power of word and music in mission.

prayer

God of the Dance,
we turn to you in praise and thanksgiving.
Help us never to be ashamed
to proclaim your glory.
Amen.

theological reflection

The heavens declare thy glory, Lord;
    in every star thy wisdom shines;
but when our eyes behold thy word,
    we read thy name in fairer lines.

Sun, moon and stars convey thy praise
   round the whole earth, and never stand;
so, when thy truth began its race,
   it touched and glanced on every land.

Nor shall thy spreading Gospel rest
   till through the world thy truth has run;
till Christ has all the nations blest
   that see the light or feel the sun.

Great Sun of Righteousness, arise;
   bless the dark world with heavenly light;
thy Gospel makes the simple wise,
   thy laws are pure, thy judgements right.

Thy noblest wonders here we view,
   in souls renewed and sins forgiven:
Lord, cleanse my sins, my soul renew,
   and make thy word my guide to heaven.[1]

Isaac Watts was born over 250 years ago and wrote hymns that are collected in many of the different hymn books used in our churches. Yet his hymns can still help us focus on important questions in the Church about how Christian theology comes to people through worship. Beyond that, an important question for mission is how people become attached to their favourite hymns and why it is that words and music come to resonate with desires, hopes and loves. This is something on which Christian ministers will often reflect with people when planning a baptism, marriage or funeral service. Sometimes, people will choose a pop song or other music, but a great many want a special hymn, remembered from childhood or encountered at school. How do we use our great musical tradition of hymnody and singing worship songs to evoke in people a renewed sense of their own spirituality? One of the ways we might do this, is to remind ourselves of the richness of some of our great hymns.

In this hymn, for example, Isaac Watts begins from a scriptural basis in Psalm 19. A vision of the whole creation praising the Creator is evoked. Praise is seen as a characteristic of the creation: we live in a blessed, sacred world. If we see the world in this way, then we see the world as showing forth God: 'the world is filled with the grandeur of God' as Gerard Manley Hopkins has it.[2] From this way of seeing, God is not eclipsed, hidden or absent, but clearly is in relation with the whole creation.

As God's word has come into the world, so it has entered human society. Moreover, the gospel is like an energizing water flow percolating through the world. Its energy is oriented to nothing less than the whole world being blessed by Christ. Just as the sun shines on all parts of the planet, so the hymn asks God to give us a greater, spiritual light. In this light, the kingdom is established where 'laws are pure' and 'judgements right'. The injustices and flaws of the human condition are addressed and removed.

In the last verse, Isaac Watts returns to what this means to the individual. In contemplating the creation, and in the context of God's purposes, we can see ourselves as wishing to turn to Christ and to make a commitment. We ask for renewal and forgiveness and a way of living that allows us to contemplate our ultimate destiny: life with God in eternity.

some thoughts from the group

We enjoyed singing together and realized what a different kind of conversation singing or making music together can bring about. In wondering whether the tunes or the words had more of an impact on people ('All my hope on God is founded' did not become popular until it was set to music by Herbert Howells), we thought about music as a way of bringing the gospel into other cultures. For example, one of us had had direct experience of a great growth in the churches in China because of a powerful love of the hymns and the music. Further, hymns like this one can lead us back to their foundation in scripture. One of us remembered singing hymns in primary school and then having to discuss what the words meant, and having been stumped by the word 'ineffable'! But when the words were explained and the hymn sung again, there seemed to be more richness and depth in the way the hymn could be expressed. We thought that there was a particular link between mission and worship because hymns are important to people, and special experiences, such as the joy of getting married, can be linked up to them.

We also thought about how hymns can have other functions. In Zambia, one of us had had experience of a youth choir singing an admonition to the Mothers' Union and to the priests in that place. The singing took the form of a critique, which was then answered in dialogue by the elderly. This dynamic kind of musical dialogue is in stark contrast to those places where the vicar or the choir operates a stranglehold on the music in a particular church!

Music and hymn singing is a fundamental part of our musical tradition, heritage and our liturgical celebration. But perhaps we have not exploited its mission potential, especially in exploring with people why certain hymns move or excite them.

poem: the gospel of the song

In the beginning were the Words,
    and the Words were the Poet's,
    and were part of Him:
    lively and brilliant.

And the Words become music,
    and were sung,
    full of beauty and freedom.

We have heard the Song,
    and been utterly moved,
    again and again.

We had read poetry before,
    but beauty and freedom
    came through this Song.

No one has ever seen the Poet:
    this one Song, which is in His heart,
    has shown Him to us.[3]

Graham Kings

other pathways for exploration

illustration, image or focus of meditation

Look at a musical image, listen to some quiet music, sing 'The heavens declare thy glory Lord', say Psalm 19 or use any other appropriate hymn of praise.

a purpose and a challenge

To think about the place of praise in our lives and its relationship to mission. Is praise a private matter for church or do we feel comfortable praising God in our daily lives?

some wider questions for discussion

● As Christians in mission, do we ever think about how praise can be a witness to others?

- What is the worship like in our church? How could it be improved? Does praise have to be loud and noisy? What other kinds of praise are there?

- How can the worship of God become a part of daily life? In what ways do we express our thanks to God? Does the language of the hymns (modern/traditional; inclusive/non-inclusive) make a difference to how we can use them? How?

some suggested passages for Bible study

1 Samuel 2.1-10
1 Chronicles 16.7-36
Psalm 148
Luke 2.8-20

meditation or music

All my hope on God is founded;
He doth still my faith renew.
Me through change and chance he guideth,
Only good and only true.
God unknown,
He alone
Calls my heart to be his own.

(tune 'Michael')
Robert Bridges, 'All my Hope on God is Founded'[4]

some thoughts about mission

How do we share praise with others? Do we enable the power and strength of hymns to touch people's lives and how do we engage people through favourite music, songs, hymns and prayers?

further resources

Ian Bradley, *Abide with Me – the world of Victorian hymns*, SCM, 1997. Timothy Dudley-Smith, *Flame of Love – A Personal Choice of Charles Wesley's Verse*, Triangle, 2001. Peter Harvey, *Glory, Laud and Honour*, SPCK, 1996.
Films: *Shine* (directed by Scott Hicks, Ronin Films, 1996). Fatboy Slim, 'Praise You'[5] (includes the prize-winning video of ordinary people dancing in a public place, for this track).

chapter 4

hope

Albert
Herbert,
*Jonah and
the Whale*,
c.1988.

We used the paintings in Sister Wendy's book, *The Gaze of Love*,
to focus on the mystery of death and our hope in Jesus Christ.

prayer

Creator God,
you have painted the whole creation in its richness;
you see us as we truly are.
Help us to see beyond our broken world
and know the truth and beauty you reveal to us.
Amen.

theological reflection

Sister Wendy Beckett, *The Gaze of Love*, *Meditations on Art*,
Marshall Pickering, 1993.

The real difficulty about prayer is that it has no difficulty. Prayer is God's taking possession of us. We can expose to Him what we are, and He gazes on us with the creative eye of Holy Love. His gaze is transforming: He does not leave us in our poverty but draws into being all we are meant to become. What that is we can never know. Total Love sees us in total truth because it is only He who sees us totally. Nobody else can ever know us through and through, know why we are what we are, what inherited weaknesses and strengths we have, or what wounds or insights have come to us from our upbringing. (p. 9)

Sister Wendy is known to the general public as a contemplative nun, as an art historian and also as a television presenter whose gift is for explaining works of art in terms of their richness of idea and meaning to people without the specialized knowledge necessary for the deep contemplation of painting. In *The Gaze of Love*, she finds a wealth of spiritual insight in 40 paintings and offers her theological reflection on each of the subjects.

This book was the special companion of Corinna,[1] after she was diagnosed with a widespread cancer. Corinna had had a Christian upbringing, but was not a churchgoer and was not supported by a Christian community. She had spent her life bringing up a large family and on a typical Sunday she cooked a big roast dinner for everyone and spent the day making sure everyone was fed and all their needs catered for. She had no special interest in art, finding much of it incomprehensible, but was devoted to Sister Wendy after seeing her on television.

From the beginning of her illness, Corinna was required to make complicated choices about treatments. She had a course of chemotherapy during which her hair fell out and she developed painful infections in her mouth and throat, which made it difficult to swallow. She lost weight and became weak and frail. She had radiotherapy, which left her skin red, intensely sore and damaged. She felt she was trapped in a world of doctors and treatments in which her Christian faith was of little use in making decisions. She, who saw herself as a robust and healthy person, was forced to live in a world of perpetual pain. It was then that the words of Sister Wendy, above, helped her to refocus her prayer life and consider her future rather than her present. When the doctors and her family looked at her, they saw her disintegration and loss of all that she had been: healthy, active, beautiful. But Sister Wendy reminded Corinna that God sees us continually as the whole creations we are meant to be: 'He does not leave us in our poverty but draws us into being all we are meant to become' (p. 9). As she was dying, Corinna was able to focus on the promise that God knows us totally. The doctors and nurses could only deal with the part of her that was a person dying of cancer, but God was already holding her as a complete and perfect person.

The last painting in this book is Albert Herbert's *Jonah and the Whale* (c.1988). Of this dramatic picture, Sister Wendy writes:

> . . . the colours of the picture, gleaming, thick radiant, tell us something more. Jonah's dilemma is in his own mind. God's love awaits him on every side. If he lifts his eyes in prayer, he will see the sheer beauty of the Love that encompasses him. We are not asked to bear the burden of humanity alone. We are only asked to realize that alone we cannot bear it. God bears it – Jesus draws us into the Spirit of Holiness. Our only task is to ask for His help. How it will come is not our affair. Love may carry us inside a whale or along a stony shore: it may seem anything but what we want. But if we trust our God, if we accept that Jesus knew His Mystery and taught us to call Him Father, then the gleaming beauty that Herbert shows us becomes our vision of life, and there is no more fear.[2]

For Corinna, this meditation helped her to find the thread of her faith in the midst of her suffering. Her illness and approaching death were certainly not what she wanted, but the suggestion that God's love was still supporting her in ways not determined by courses of treatment, or even by the course of the cancer, helped her to deal with the feelings of helplessness and fear.

Above all, the picture itself, in which a tiny, helpless, sad, figure stands inside the mouth of a black monster, more snake than whale, gave Corinna a way to speak and pray about her own situation. The naïve form of the figures took her back to Sunday school and the place of her last experience of Christian nurture. She identified with Herbert's Jonah, a person called to fulfil a vocation, but trying to run away from all it implied – the journey through treatments and hospitals to death. She saw the black monster as the form of her cancer, holding her in its jaws, ready to engulf her, but also to deliver her. The picture provided her with ways to visualize her fears, but also to find new descriptions for her response in faith. Eventually, Corinna was able to decide that she had had enough treatment and, shortly after, died.

some thoughts from the group

Many of us have lost loved ones from cancer or know people close to us who are currently suffering from cancer. Looking at the pictures alongside Sister Wendy's comments brought back some of our most poignant memories about the death of family members, but also helped us to remember that sometimes we can allow the world's imperfections to seem all that there is. One of us remembered that her dying father had drawn a picture of himself within concentric circles, broken open by a shaft of God's love. Sometimes we blame God for the fact that we cannot always make the world a better place, but forget that God is reconciling the whole creation to God's self. We have said in the group that mission requires transformation to come into the world, but we are reminded by Sister Wendy that if we presuppose what that transformation must look like then we forget that we must be obedient to God's will and not follow our own desires.

We were impressed by what Sister Wendy says about prayer. It is easy to be cerebral about the missionary task and to spend a great deal of time analysing it and making plans, but the great thing about mission is that at the most basic level there is no difficulty about it. be a Christian is to be a missionary, to testify to Christ by our living and being.

This prayer was uttered spontaneously by Corinna's daughter upon leaving the hospital after visiting her mother. Her companion wrote it down in this form:

poem

I would like to give up my faith in you
because you do not melt the broken asphalt
You do not crush the concrete to bright powder
and pluck my mother from her dying bed

I would like to turn my back on you
because you up the stakes on every bargain
because you weigh the scales and find us wanting
because this world's a dandelion clock

I would like to tell you you aren't listening
leaving me to struggle on my own
I would like to shut and lock the Bible
and make the lonely journey on my own

Something in me will not let me leave
Something in me will not let me grieve
Something heart deep won't leave me alone
You will be there when I make it home.

other pathways for exploration

illustration, image, or focus of meditation

Albert Herbert's *Jonah and the Whale*, or other modern painting or abstract image. Or take a trip to a local art gallery or exhibition.

a purpose and a challenge

To consider the beauty of the creation. Does coping with the ugliness of pain, disease and death distract us from God's perfect will for us?

some wider questions for discussion

● As Christians in mission, how can we help others to discover the beauty of God's creation?
  Do we get distracted by the imperfection of the world?

● What does our society say about ideals of human beauty in magazines and films?
  How is this different from God's knowledge and love of ourselves?

● How do we help others to see themselves as always loved and desired by God?
  In what ways can painting or other artistic media inspire us to share our faith?

some suggested passages for Bible study

Genesis 2.4-9
Matthew 6.25-34
1 Corinthians 13.8-13

meditation or music

O God, our help in ages past,
    our hope for years to come,
our shelter from the stormy blast,
    and our eternal home;

Isaac Watts, 'O God our help in ages past'[3]

some thoughts about mission

Do we see the world as cursed and struggling under the burden of sin, or as blessed, loved and desired by God? How can we acknowledge injustice, disease and death while holding out the beauty of the creation to others? Can our efforts in mission resolve this tension?

further resources

Sister Wendy, *1000 Masterpieces*, Dorling Kindersley, 1999.
John Diamond, *C*, Vermilion, 1998.
Gillian Rose, *Love's Work*, Vintage, 1997.
David Ford, *The Shape of Living*, HarperCollins (Fount), 1997.
Nicholas Woltersdorff, *Lament for a Son*, Eerdmans, 1987.
Film: *Iris* (directed by Richard Eyre, Buena Vista International/Miramax, 2001).

chapter 5

the cross

We used a picture of Jonathan Clarke's sculpture *The Eighth Hour* to focus once again on the crucified body of Christ.

prayer

Loving God,
you have given us your son Jesus Christ
to die upon a cross.
For some he is a victor, for some a victim,
for some the only hope in hopelessness.
When we look upon the cross,
let us remember the pouring out of your love
uniquely given.
Amen.

theological reflection

Lo! I will declare the best of dreams which I dreamt in the
middle of the night, when human creatures lay at rest. It seemed
to me that I saw a wondrous tree rising aloft, encompassed with
light, the brightest of crosses. All that sign was overlaid with gold;
fair jewels were set at the surface of the cross-beam. All the
angels of God, fair by creation, looked on there; verily that was
no malefactor's cross, but holy spirits gazed on Him there, men
upon earth and all this glorious universe.[1]

When we look upon this five-foot tall sculpture of Jesus on the cross
by Jonathan Clarke,[2] our first impression could be of an eagle or a bird-
man. If you look more closely at the sculpture, you can see that Christ
is not only on the cross but also *in* the cross. This is a muscular Christ
made of aluminium, whereas the cross is made of rough oak. The arms
are twisted in three directions and the body also is twisted. Many
different things can be seen in it. It reminds the onlooker of the story
of Samson in Judges 16.29-30 when he brought down the pillars of
the temple. In verse 30, we are told that Samson killed more people in
death than during his life; but Jesus on the cross saved more people
by his death than in his earthly life.

Another interesting thing about the sculpture is that the process
by which it was begun involved carving the image in polystyrene
with a hot wire. The molten aluminium is poured into the mould
and vaporizes it, so that the mould is lost, never to be used again.
This means that the image is unique. This might remind us of the
flimsiness of this world in relation to the solidity of the next, the
'solid joys and lasting treasure'[3] we are promised. So, in the sculpture
we see the solid aluminium emerging from the flimsy mould that will
not stand up to the heat. Therefore there is also a death and
resurrection in the making of the sculpture itself.

The sculpture also shows Christ aggressively taking on the evil of
the world and fighting it. He is simultaneously fighting evil and yet
being vanquished by it. Christ is also overcome by the cross that
is encroaching upon him, and this might remind us of the women
touching Jesus, pressing upon him and constraining him. Yet, although
death appears to win, Jesus defeats death. He puts the evil out of
circulation by absorbing it himself.

some thoughts from the group

We were impressed by learning about the way the sculpture had been manufactured. The annihilation of the mould should give us cause to ponder the meaning of death and resurrection. We were also reminded that the divine creativity is not constrained by our human ideas about being, thinking and doing. Above all, the creation of the figure of Christ and the annihilation of the mould reminded us of the choice for all who are offered the Christian story – will we follow Christ or turn away from him?

One of the things with which the cross faces us is the idea of human freedom as a choice of turning away from or turning to God. It follows from this that there is a possibility of eternally turning away from or turning to God and that without these possibilities there is no point in human freedom. Does judgement include a reversal of creation: if we came out of nothing, then can we go back to nothing?

So what might it mean for us in mission when people say 'no' to God? What do we think happens then? One understanding is that if human beings say no to God and are judged eternally, then it follows that they must die eternally. But judgement could mean that human beings have separated eternally from God but that they might continue to exist. Yet we remembered that Origen[4] has a vision of the end of time with the devil and the angels where everything is sustained in existence by God in love, in order not to lose those he has created. Further, theologians such as Karl Rahner[5] have suggested that those who say no will ultimately be overwhelmed by the power of God's love. We differed in our thoughts about this, but we noted that the Bible has a tradition of God sustaining people in love who have, none the less, said no. We see this in John 13 where Jesus still holds out possibilities to Judas. Yet Judas still goes out into the night. What about those who never have the chance to respond to God's invitation? Some people never have the freedom to make such a choice. If people can be eternally lost, does God not then lament their loss eternally?

Many people are not attracted by God yet, in Revelation, the gates are always open. Are there those who will never come into the city? It makes a difference to our view of mission: is the invitation here and now all there is for people, or does God's grace continually offer us choice, even beyond death? Gazing on Jonathan Clarke's sculpture we were reminded again that the wounds of Christ are important in heaven.[6]

poem: the first written gospel

Jesus the Sacred, tried before Pilate;
Pilate the scared – trial before Caesar:
Jesus, entitled to justice from Rome,
entitled by Pilate 'The King of the Jews.'

First written Gospel, translated for all,
title deeds of the Kingdom of God;
proclaimed to the city, unchanging Word,
'What is written is written', bequeathed to the world.

Graham Kings

other pathways for exploration

illustration, image or focus of meditation

Use the reproduction of Jonathan Clarke's sculpture or any cross in the church, the home or piece of jewellery. Do any of these have a history or other story to tell?

a purpose and a challenge

Look again at the crucifixion. Are we so familiar with the idea of preaching Christ crucified that we have forgotten the power, drama, horror and joy of what happened on the cross?

some wider questions for discussion

● As Christians in mission, how might we tell the story of the crucifixion to others who have no grounding in Christian tradition?

● Has our society turned the cross into a mere fashion accessory? If so, say how.
How do we relate the importance of the crucifixion to our own faith?

● How does the image of the cross relate to events in our own lives? What does it mean to have one who was crucified as both God and human being at the heart of our faith?

some suggested passages for Bible study

Judges 16.28-30
Luke 23.32-46
Romans 6.1-11

meditation or music

When I survey the wondrous Cross
    on which the Prince of Glory died,
my richest gain I count but loss,
    and pour contempt on all my pride.

          Isaac Watts, 'When I survey the wondrous cross'[7]

some thoughts about mission

Does God's invitation to people ever run out? Do we have a picture of heaven that includes only those we would find it comfortable meeting there? How does the cross help us to make sense of eternal life in Christ?

further resources

David Atkinson, *God so Loved the World: Towards a Missionary Theology*, SPCK, 1999.
William Golding, *Pincher Martin*, Faber, 1956.
Film: *The Mission*[8]
Music: U2, 'In the name of Love' (from the album *The Unforgettable Fire*, Island Records, 1984).

chapter 6

evil

Susan White,
*Woman
oppressed*,
Gosford sand-
stone, 1989.

In this reflection, we used a disturbing and difficult Bible story to think about the presence of evil in the world and our reactions to it.

prayer

Compassionate God,
you weep for the suffering in your creation;
you see injustice, cruelty and evil.
Help us not to hide our faces from this pain,
but seek to hold and heal all who cry for help.
Amen.

theological reflection

Judges 19–21: a story of abuse and terror.

In those days, when there was no king in Israel, a certain
Levite, residing in the remote parts of the hill country of Ephraim,
took to himself a concubine from Bethlehem in Judah. But his
concubine became angry with him, and she went away from
him to her father's house at Bethlehem in Judah, and was there
some four months. Then her husband set out after her, to speak
tenderly to her and bring her back . . .

While they were enjoying themselves, the men of the city, a
perverse lot, surrounded the house and started pounding on the
door. They said to the old man, the master of the house, 'Bring
out the man who came into your house, so that we may have
intercourse with him.' And the man, the master of the house,
went out to them and said to them, 'No, my brothers, do not act
so wickedly. Since this man is my guest, do not do this vile thing.
Here are my virgin daughter and his concubine; let me bring them
out now. Ravish them and do whatever you want to them; but
against this man do not do such a vile thing.' But the men would
not listen to him. So the man seized his concubine, and put her
out to them. They wantonly raped her, and abused her all through
the night until the morning. And as the dawn began to break, they
let her go. As morning appeared, the woman came and fell down
at the door of the man's house where her master was, until it
was light.

In the morning her master got up, opened the doors of the house,
and when he went to go on his way, there was the concubine lying
at the door of the house, with her hands on the threshold. 'Get up,'
he said to her, 'we are going.' But there was no answer. Then he put
her on the donkey; and the man set out for his home. When he had
entered his house, he took a knife, and grasping his concubine he
cut her in twelve pieces, limb by limb, and sent her throughout all
the territory of Israel.

This is the story of an owned woman who only ever commits one action
under her own control, that is, to run home, away from her owner, the
Levite. After this, she is entirely under the control of others, who deal
with her as a piece of property and, in the end, rape her to death. It
is clear that her father does not want to relinquish her back into the
hands of the Levite, but his rights over his daughter will only allow him

to delay the departure by extending his hospitality. In the end, the Levite takes his concubine and sets off.

The hospitality of his next host has fatal consequences. When the mob howls for the sexual use of his guest, the host will not permit such a breach of hospitality. No, the women are offered instead, first the host's own virgin daughter, then the concubine. Verses 26-28a are desperately poignant. The concubine has been brutally abused, raped all night long and at dawn makes her way back to her only safety. There she is found, dead, in the morning, with her hands reaching out to the threshold, where even that last refuge was denied her.

The Levite has suffered a terrible insult in the loss of his concubine. He dismembers her and sends the parts as a horrible call to the twelve tribes to avenge the outrage. Immediately, the men start posturing. The tribe of Benjamin is unprepared to give up the perpetrators of the deed, and the situation degenerates into an orgy of killing. After the killing, the tribes face a dreadful consequence. Part of their posturing was an oath that none of the other eleven tribes would give their daughters to marry Benjaminites. Yet, because of the slaughter, which included women and children as well as men, the tribe was now not in a position to regenerate itself and was in danger of being lost. The very identity of Israel, with its twelve tribes, was at risk. Well, but we only said we would not *give* our daughters. What if they were *stolen*?

This was the plan. During the coming religious festival, the girls and young women would all be dancing. Suppose the Benjaminite men were alerted to this, and given to understand that there would be only token resistance if they took the women by force? The plan worked! The young women were seized by force. The identity of Israel was saved and honour was satisfied. This terrible story from the book of Judges bears out the experience of many survivors of abuse, and we learn important lessons about how abuse can happen today.

Although women may be at the centre of their own experience, the context here is a story of male prestige, hierarchy and power. Often, the woman's only possible action is to flee to a male protector. The male protector may then not have the power to offer protection, or may be part of the abusive network.

In the end, abusive male structures can be more interested in preserving their own identity and power than in protecting the women, whom they have stripped of the power to protect themselves. These structures make women dependent, then turn out not to be dependable.

Families, workplaces and churches are capable of lying and cheating in order to preserve their dignity and hide abuse from themselves. Just as the Israelites found a deceitful way round their self-imposed oath, which put women at yet further indignity and risk, so abusive structures will plan to sacrifice the vulnerable in order to preserve a semblance of honour. Of course not all victims are women, nor all perpetrators men. Not all power structures are male. However, this particular scriptural story illustrates a very common pattern of abuse in all its complexity. Neither are all women victims or all men perpetrators. Elsewhere in scripture women and men are seen to live and work in non-abusive relationships, in which the honour and dignity of all are upheld, and there is a proper distribution of power. This can be seen particularly in the attitude of Jesus to women and men, whom he treated equally as fully human participants in living, with needs to be met and gifts to offer.

some thoughts from the group

We try to have hearts for mission in a world where terrible things take place and in which people are often bewildered and confused by the magnitude of hatred and evil, which seem to occur everywhere. Into the newspapers and television reports of suffering and abuse, we must bring God's message of joy and hope. Yet this is not a simple redress of suffering and pain, but a warning to ourselves to live lives worthy of scrutiny. This means we have to be aware of how we behave in the Church and of the important relationship between mission and Christian ethics. Often people accuse the Church of hypocrisy, pointing to times when people in the Church have caused harm to others. Perhaps we must try to remember that scripture embraces terrible stories of rape and murder, suffering and tragedy, as well as joy and hope, yet often we duck the difficult issues these raise and stick to the uplifting stories that make us feel good. Where in the Church do we deal effectively with abuse and with injustice and how far does that become part of our outreach, our desire to act transformatively in our own situation? What do we *really* think about the presence of sin in the world and God's response of forgiveness to our penitence? Is this something we are prepared to offer to others as part of our mission work, or does it come with conditions?

poem: revolutionary love

Turning the world upside down,
is the charge against Silas and Paul:
turning its values the right way up,
is the Kingdom's promise and call.

Invitations to a glorious feast
mean more to the hungry and poor,
and to others who have the least,
than to the rich, well known and well fed,
who prefer their own company instead.

Love for those who like you is ordinary;
love for those who are like you, narcissistic;
love for those who are unlike you, extraordinary;
love for those who dislike you, revolutionary.

Revenge surrenders to evil by reflecting violence:
but, like a bad coin kept and not passed on,
like lightning conducted safely to earth,
love neutralises evil, by absorbing violence.

Pray for the rival who threatens you;
pray for the adversary blocking you;
pray for the opponent who slanders you;
pray for the antagonist provoking you.

You only love the Father
as much as you love your worst enemy.
For your love is to be merciful and free,
indiscriminate, spontaneous,
uncalculatingly generous;
when all is said and done –
like Father, like Son.

Graham Kings

other paths for exploration

illustration, image or focus of meditation

An image associated with victims, perhaps from a newspaper
photograph. Posters or an art image of the Virgin holding the dead
Christ may also be appropriate.

a purpose and a challenge

To think about the presence of evil in the world and how we make sense of it. Do we avoid the darker side of human nature and ignore the challenges it poses in our own lives?

some wider questions for discussion

- As Christians in mission, how do we respond to the suffering of others, including where people in the Church have done harm? How do we make sense of terrible crimes against human beings?

- In what ways can we care for those suffering in our community? What kinds of pastoral care, liturgy, healing or other action can we offer?

- How do we feel about those who perpetrate abuse? Does our society, especially through the use of the Internet, make it easier for us to abuse others?

suggested passages for Bible study

2 Samuel 13.1-23
Job 1.13-21
John 8.3-11

meditation

'No Father. I've a very different idea of love. And until my dying day I shall refuse to love a scheme of things in which children are put to torture.'

A shade of disquietude crossed the priest's face. He was silent a moment. Then, 'Ah, doctor,' he said sadly, 'I've just realized what is meant by "grace".'[1]

some thoughts about mission

Our task as Christians is not just to overwhelm people with God's love, but to be alongside, to hold and sustain those who suffer. We have to seek to provide a space for the voice of the voiceless to be heard, the victim to be acknowledged.

further resources

Stephen Parsons, *Ungodly Fear,* Lion Books, 2000.

Lawrence Osborn and Andrew Walker, *Harmful Religion: an exploration of religious abuse*, SPCK, 1997.

Christian Survivors of Sexual Abuse. See www.mtb1.demon.co.uk/cssa/cssa.htm.

Frazer Watts, Rebecca Nye and Sara Savage, *Psychology for Christian Ministry*, Routledge, 2002.

Lynne Price, 'Maggots in the luggage' in Simon Barrow and Graeme Smith, eds, *Christian Mission in Western Society*, CTBI, 2001.

Films: *Sleeping with the Enemy* (directed by Joseph Ruben, 20th Century Fox, 2001); *The Accused* (directed by Jonathan Kaplan, Paramount, 1998).

chapter 7
absence

We considered a poem by R. S. Thomas to make connections between our situation at the beginning of the twenty-first century, the two thousand years of Christian tradition and the eternal and unchanging presence of God in creation.

prayer

God of light and shadow,
sometimes when we look for you
it seems you are gone from us,
gone on a journey, or sleeping, or far away.
Help us to remember that the fire fell from heaven,
because of faith. Let that faith be ours.
Amen.

theological reflection

'The Moon in Lleyn'

The last quarter of the moon
of Jesus gives way
to the dark; the serpent
digests the egg. Here
on my knees in this stone
church, that is full only
of the silent congregation
of shadows and the sea's
sound, it is easy to believe
Yeats was right. Just as though
choirs had not sung, shells
have swallowed them; the tide laps
at the Bible; the bell fetches
no people to the brittle miracle
of the bread. The sand is waiting
for the running back of the grains
in the wall into its blond
glass. Religion is over, and
what will emerge from the body
of the new moon, no one
can say.
            But a voice sounds
in my ear: Why so fast,
mortal? These very seas
are baptised. The parish
has a saint's name time cannot
unfrock. In cities that
have outgrown their promise people
are becoming pilgrims
again, if not to this place,
then to the recreation of it
in their own spirits. You must remain
kneeling. Even as this moon
making its way through the earth's
cumbersome shadow, prayer, too,
has its phases.[1]

For some people today, God has gone missing or seems absent.
In such a fast-changing world as this, an ever-constant, unchanging
God may seem impossible. Our contemporary society has lost some
things on which we, as Christians, have formerly relied: a foundational
knowledge of scripture and a tradition of going to church. This has

left many people adrift with questions that cannot be answered. For example, a young woman on a train was heard to ask: 'Why is it called "Good Friday"'? Is it because it is a good night on television?' On being told why we have a Good Friday in the Christian tradition, she was amazed that she had never heard such an extraordinary story and at first refused to believe that it could be true. It seemed so astonishing, so very far from a 'good night on the TV'. In the face of this loss, we can understand why for one elderly priest 'the last quarter of the moon of Jesus gives way to the dark'. In some churches, the faith seems to be dying, just because people are no longer coming faithfully as they once did, on a Sunday.

Yet, R. S. Thomas reminds us that these are but small pictures of a local situation. We can be caught up in the idea that our own time is the only time and that our sense of the 'now' is the most important. For people who are working ever harder in difficult rural or urban areas, where perhaps elderly congregations are dwindling, or the community is struggling, then it is easy to become discouraged and forget God's larger purposes. We should not forget the legacy of Christian commitment and prayer that has carried the Church to the twenty-first century. This history and powerful memory is still significant: 'the parish has a saint's name time cannot unfrock'. There is still strong connectedness to the holy. People too, continue to have a desperate spiritual hunger and are searching for value, purpose and meaning in their lives; they turn their faces towards God without necessarily knowing what or whom they seek. Our missionary purpose is, therefore, also centred in maintaining the tradition through prayer, reading scripture, worship and celebration of the sacraments. We also have a part in helping those who search for the truth in the history of our faith, and to make it known. R. S. Thomas reminds us of the larger Christian hope, that if we seem to move into a dark phase, perhaps in the fortunes of our own parish at a particular time, so we know we will again move into the light. We should not be surprised by this, for it is written into how nature itself works. We will see this if we remain faithful, constant and hopeful of God's eternal purposes. This should be a source of encouragement to us.

some thoughts from the group

In thinking about this, we considered the resurgent interest in Celtic spirituality. This is not necessarily a return to some 'authentic' form of worship from an earlier time, but points to a desire to recover the spirit of faith, sharing and prayer that fired Christians in the earlier history of our islands. Some of the interest in Celtic spirituality comes from a desire for a more inclusive, less hierarchical approach to being church. Another attraction is its creative way of approaching scripture, liturgy and sharing in community. Alongside this, we find Christians longing to express a desire to recover the sense of the sacredness of creation, of holy places and spaces, and a further holistic sense of the world as blessed, loved and desired by God.

We thought that, just as R. S. Thomas realizes that our human structures, edifices and buildings are as nothing before the sand and the sea, so we should stand back and try to gain a perspective on the patience of God. We are often so *impatient* with God and try to push our understanding of the divine will into our own time frames and perceptions.

We decided that there is a place in mission for waiting on God, keeping the rumour and memory of God alive and for realizing that our work and witness may be about maintaining the faith in places where the Christian presence seems all but to have departed. Yet, where 'people are becoming pilgrims again', our own faithfulness is tested. Are we always journeying too, and ready to reveal to people the source of our hope?

poem: coracle prayer

Lord Jesus Christ,
teacher on the shore
   who calls and overwhelms us,
friend in the boat
   who sleeps and saves us,
mystery on the water
   who prays and surprises us,
stranger on the other shore
   who rises to welcome us,
guide our coracle across. Amen.

Graham Kings

other pathways for exploration

illustration, image or focus of meditation

Any wild or desolate landscape scene, or painting by Craigie Aitchison, for example.

a purpose and a challenge

To think about how the culture of success affects the Church. Are full churches the only goal of mission? What happens when churches are struggling for survival and God seems far away?

some wider questions for discussion

● As Christians in mission, is the aim to fill the church? What are the hallmarks of a 'successful' church or of a 'missionary congregation'?

● Must the Church prepare for a time of exile? What does the theme of exile in the Bible tell us about faithfulness to God in dark times?

● Have there been times when you have felt it difficult to be close to God, or that God is absent or missing from life? What does it feel like when faith is shaken?

suggested passages for Bible study

Psalm 77
Lamentations 1.1-5
Mark 15.33-39

meditation or music

By the Waters of Delivery
By breathing and brooding
by breaking and birthing
by parting and loosing
by stirring and soothing:

By giving, re-living
by stilling, refreshing
by drowning, immersing
by raising, re-versing

you, Lord, deliver us.

                                    Graham Kings

further resources

Michael Nazir-Ali, *Shapes of the Church to Come*, Kingsway, 2001.
Matthew Arnold, 'Dover Beach' in *Matthew Arnold, Selected Poems and Prose*, edited by Denys Thompson, Heinemann,1971, pp. 72–73.
Robert Warren, *Building Missionary Congregations*, Church House Publishing, 1995.
David Wood, *Poet, Priest and Prophet: Bishop John V. Taylor,* CTBI, 2002.

chapter 8
loss

We used Barbara Kingsolver's novel to look at what happens when the Gospel comes into contact with other cultures, and at appropriate and inappropriate evangelism.

theological reflection

Barbara Kingsolver, *The Poisonwood Bible*, Faber edition, 1999.

This awful night is the worst we've ever known: the *nsongonya*. They came on us like a nightmare. Nelson bang-bang-banging on the door got tangled up with my sleep, so that, even after I was awake, the next hours had the unsteady presence of a dream. Before I even knew where I was, I found myself pulled along by somebody's hand in the dark and a horrible fiery sting sloshing up my calves. We were wading through very hot water, I thought, but it couldn't be water, so I tried to ask the name of the burning liquid that had flooded our house – no, for we were already outside – that had flooded the whole world.

Ants. We were walking on, surrounded, enclosed, enveloped, eaten by *ants.* Every surface was covered and boiling, and the path like black flowing lava in the moonlight. Dark, bulbous tree trunks seethed and bulged. The grass had become a field of dark daggers standing upright, churning and crumpling in on themselves. We walked on ants and ran on them, releasing their vinegary smell to the weird, quiet night. (p. 349)

The narrator here is Leah, daughter of a Southern Baptist preacher, strong in his faith and in his mission and sent to bring the Good News to the people of the Belgian Congo on the eve of their turbulent independence (perhaps an ironic background in the light of subsequent events in the Democratic Republic of Congo). She discovers the hard way what happens to the absolute-truth claims of the Christian gospel in alien contexts. Her father has been preaching hellfire and damnation for all who hear the word of God and do not respond to it; he is consumed by uncompromising prophetic zeal, but when hellfire comes it takes not only the people he views as ignorant heathen but his own God-fearing family with it. Hell comes in the form of fire ants, devouring all before them. The people are caught up in the fiery lake, but it is not the Christians who know how to escape it. When the ants have passed through, destroying all in their path, they have cleaned out the preacher's house as surely as Sodom and Gomorrah were destroyed. Only the bones of the domestic animals are left, picked entirely clean. The Christian home is not spared, indeed the house is purified. If we call down judgement then surely we too shall be judged. What the preacher fails to connect with is that the indigenous word *bangala*, which means 'good', or 'great' also means when inflected differently, 'poisonwood', the thing you don't touch with a bargepole unless you want to suffer. So 'Jesus is *Bangala*', simultaneously means two opposing things, and both are true for the people in different situations.

In our sophisticated western culture we often think we can control everything, including nature, but we cannot. We can clone Dolly the sheep, but we cannot control the virulent contagion of foot-and-mouth disease. Similarly, we tend to think that earthquakes and tidal waves and tornadoes happen somewhere out there to cause trouble to other humans, but we forget that our place on the planet is among, not doing to. Everything is *not* under our control. So the fire ants ask a difficult question of us: will we know what to do when the fire comes? *Why should we expect to be spared?*

If we are equipping people for mission then we have to consider whether we are also equipping them to go to hell, for hell comes in many forms for many people. We know all too well about the effects of war and violence, poverty and famine, disease and distress. Often we forget that Christian tradition talks about Christ's harrowing of hell. He rescues the people from the flames and sets them free. Mission then can include being alongside people in the flames. Social justice demands that we walk into the flames alongside our brothers and sisters, not just view the smoke from far off.

some thoughts from the group

Barbara Kingsolver's narrative raised for us the issue of control in the Church, which can become a central issue in the way we live out our faith. For example, in the foot-and-mouth outbreak, farmers felt helpless, but some Christians were wondering why prayer and righteousness do not change things. Sometimes Christians become 'control freaks', feeling that Christian ministry is about control – of congregations and of God. However, the crucifixion does not fit with this. The loss of control is signalled by the earthquake and the darkness. The descent into hell begins in Gethsemane. In this respect we can learn from Christians living in countries that have suffered natural disasters like earthquakes and where they have had to ask 'Where is God in the context of these huge uncontrollable events that cost people's lives?' Perhaps, to equip ourselves for mission, we need to understand what it is like not to be in control, and to see the Spirit of God moving unfettered through the world. This can feel both risky and scary. But mission is about risking all for God.

For example, the Columbans encourage new lay missionaries to go to areas where they have not been before, in order to obtain new experiences. This is precisely an exercise in learning to have no control. One young woman, for instance, went into a hospice. Her vibrant, energetic life was taken into the arena of the dying. Another teacher went into a Harmondsworth detention centre where most of the people did not speak English. This person had a great deal of experience of using words but, in this environment, there were no words. What do we learn from losing our control and feeling powerless and how does this help us to be more missionary?

poem: facing the image

Formed in the image and likeness of God,
    we rejoice;
fired by violence and facing away,
    we recoil;
defaced, despairing, curved in on ourselves,
    we cry;
remaking, repairing, curved into the world,
    you come, the Image of God.

With compassion, forgiveness, restoring the image,
    you heal;
with powerfully piercing, incisive insight,
    you teach;
with passion and proverb and practical story,
    you preach.

Facing Jerusalem, challenging temple,
    you suffer;
surfacing from the depths of death,
    you're raised;
infusing, renewing, the image refacing,
    you pour out the fiery Spirit of God.

Being transfigured into your likeness,
    from glory to glory;
with unveiled face, we face God's Image,
    reflecting in the light of the knowledge of God
    seen in your face,
    Jesus our Lord.

Graham Kings

other paths for exploration

illustration, image or focus of meditation

Any image of the African landscape, or people.

purpose and challenge

To think about how the gospel crosses boundaries of culture.
How does encountering people from other countries challenge
and change us?

some wider questions for discussion

● As Christians in mission, do we think mission is about making others like ourselves?

● What happens when we encounter people from different faiths and cultures?

● What is the place of penitence and forgiveness in learning from our mistakes?

suggested passages for Bible study

Jeremiah 31.15-17
Matthew 13.1-17
Revelation 5.9-14

meditation

God has created me to do him some definite service;
he has committed some work to me which he has not committed to another.
I have my mission – I may never know it in this life,
but I shall know it in the next.

I have a part in this great work; I am a link in a chain, a bond of connection between persons. He has not created me for nothing, I shall do good, I shall do his work; I shall be an angel of peace, a preacher of truth in my own place, even while not intending it, if I do but keep his commandments and serve him in my calling.

Therefore I will trust him.
Whatever I am, I can never be thrown away.
If I am in sickness, my sickness can serve him;
in perplexity my perplexity may serve him.
He does nothing in vain. He knows what he is about. I do not ask to see; I do not ask to know;
I ask simply to be used.

John Henry Newman[1]

some thoughts about mission

What do we know about our mission links and partners in other countries? What can they teach us? Are we prepared to be re-evangelized by people from churches overseas?

further resources

Robert Schreiter, *Reconciliation, Mission and Ministry in a Changing Social Order*, Orbis Books, 1992.

Voices from Africa: *Transforming Mission in a Context of Marginalization* Church House Publishing, 2002.

Graham Kings, *Christianity Connected: Hindus, Muslims and the World in the letters of Max Warren and Roger Hooker*, Zoetermeer, 2002 (number 13 in the 'Mission' series).

Vincent Donovan, *Christianity Rediscovered: An Epistle from the Masai*, SCM, 1978, 1982.

chapter 9
desire

We considered the way the 'spiritual' has become a marketable commodity in our western society by focusing on the Bluewater shopping centre in Kent.

prayer

Unchanging God,
you see this world we have made for ourselves,
full of wealth, poverty, luxury and want.
Teach us to see beyond the seductions of desire
and find our satisfaction in your love.
Amen.

theological reflection

The Bluewater Shopping Centre in Kent, opened in 1999, is the largest retail shopping centre in Europe. Its stated philosophy is 'to make shopping an enjoyable, stress-free experience, and to treat all our customers as Guests'.[1] It is suggested that a day out at Bluewater can cover all a person's shopping, entertainment and leisure needs. There are all kinds of coffee bars and restaurants, catering for all tastes. There is entertainment for children, a golf course, a boating lake, as well as other occasional activities and interests. There is a cinema complex, including a special service in which wine and canapés are served before the film in a dedicated bar area. Shoppers can ask for valet parking and concierge services, and special facilities for the disabled. Yet there is only a 'quiet room', no designated chapel.[2]

Some shoppers, however, have suggested that the design and layout of Bluewater provides them with a kind of 'spiritual' experience, beyond the 'retail therapy'. The shops are laid out in three sides of a triangle so that it is possible to keep walking around the malls on a journey of discovery. Each 'side' of the triangle is different: one side has a water theme, with the course of the Thames inlaid on the floor and smoothed rocks to sit on. Another side has an earth theme, with sculptured animals and birds set into the walls, and flowers gracing the galleries. The last side has an air theme, with white suspended sails drifting from the ceiling. Around the malls run lines of poetry and different colours signal different moods. In one intersection of sides, leather sofas invite weary shoppers to sit down with a coffee and contemplate the Zodiac under a starry dome, for Bluewater is full of pathways and rest places, and the suggestion of water, light and air. Children can eat their burgers and chips in a forest and play on stepping stones across a pool. At the same time, there is always something going on, some entertainment, or new stall, so that no two visits to the shopping centre are ever quite the same. Interestingly, Bluewater also claims to orient its three different sides to different clients: the Guildhall area is for the *discerning* shopper; the Rose Gallery for *families*; the Thames Walk for the *fashion conscious*. Shops and restaurants are located in those areas that are judged to appeal most to these groups of people.

During the last few shopping days at Christmas 2001, 870,000 people visited Bluewater and spent huge amounts of money. Yet people were also attracted by the spectacle, the glitter and sparkle of decorations, the giant illuminated reindeer grazing on the grassy plots beside the car parks. A powerful sense of nostalgic Christmas was evoked, with Santa's Grotto, a carousel and Salvation Army carols. Bluewater is, therefore, an 'experience' rather than a shopping centre, in which all the senses can be engaged. Bluewater also extends its influence into the community: 'we've worked hard to be a good neighbour'. Its mission statement is: 'To proactively integrate Bluewater and the community by being sensitive to particular needs and supporting community development'. The web site news report for 19 March 2001 tells of volunteers from Bluewater helping to redecorate the Northfleet Churches' Neighbourhood Centre. Moreover, Bluewater also claims to be committed to a comprehensive Environmental Management Programme with close attention to waste management and recycling initiatives.

So: where else would you want to spend your money . . .?

some thoughts from the group

What is so attractive about Bluewater? One noticeable thing is that coffee bars open out on to the malls and the smell of coffee drifts across. Would people enjoy coming into Church more if they were greeted by a homely and hospitable smell? We noted that in other parts of the globe, the domestic and the church worlds were integrated, and the *Alpha* course also makes this connection. What then, is the significance of the kitchen, annexed to the church or as part of the church hall? Of course, we most often have coffee or refreshments *after* the service and we have had a tradition of fasting before coming to Church, so the message seems to be more about denial than hospitality. Yet in seeker-friendly worship, people have had to look at issues of common language, of the numinous, of transcendence, and of the words we use. We might think about how sights, smells and sounds as well as words communicate encounter with God.

But is there also something disquieting about Bluewater? In some sense, it sets out to be a cathedral and its architect had experience of designing cathedrals in America. Its spirituality is that of the consumer. The quiet room is also not unlocked – you need the key. Was the design and construction of Bluewater to attract consumers and to get them to spend money, a piece of social engineering? The design of Bluewater also raises questions about the mission of cathedrals. There needs to be a space and silence, but also a bright, attractive welcome. Can our great cathedrals compete with the attractions of Bluewater? Smell, colour, stillness – all these things can be significant to people who are searching for God.

Some people have negative perceptions of church, or experiences that are hollow, empty and fruitless. Yet others find fellowship in shopping together. Where do we take account of this in our witness to others? One of us told the story of arriving at a church to bless some glass doors. When he arrived, he was told that the oak outer doors of the church were shut during the services. So why were the glass doors put in? He was told the oak doors were open during the week when there was nothing going on. Is it really such a novel idea to open the church doors during the service? Bluewater is open to welcome every kind of person for long hours, yet for some, church is a private and enclosed ritual, which goes on behind closed doors.

Apart from this, we should not forget the money side of it all. There is enormous capital investment in Bluewater. Its purpose is to make money and people are encouraged to spend their money when they go there. It speaks directly to our modern culture's desire to possess material things. What happens when the 'spiritual' becomes a fashion accessory for retail therapy? And how should we respond?

poem: profit and loss

John is just the right man for the job,
which is, after all,
one of justice and righteousness.

Savile Row clothes aren't suitable,
nor is after-shave;
the dust and smell of the desert hang about him;
so do the people.

The word of the Lord, silent for so long,
at last is heard again: 'It's time to change!'

Not a polite call, in this waste land,
of 'Time, gentlemen, please';
not 'Time to leave for tomorrow is another day'
  – for it probably isn't!

But 'the crisis has come. This is it.
'Here is he who comes after me.'
Not 'you can't change the world,
that's just the way it is.'
But the specific questions 'Is it just, the way it is?'

The health of the poor in Britain rots
  improve housing and benefits;

the hunger and debt of the world mounts
  trade fairly and justly;
the inside of the stock market collapses
  deal honestly and openly;
star wars astronomically cost the earth
  be content with present defence.

His shout demands, 'Time to change
turn around, you can't go on.'
Not a casual 'Take it or leave it'
but a crucial 'Take it or be left – like the chaff.
And don't you try the old school tie;
trees are judged by fruits, not roots.'

Graham Kings

other paths for exploration

preparation

It might be interesting to organize a trip out to a large shopping centre, if practical, and ask people to make a note of their impressions.

illustration, image or focus of meditation

Information or publicity from the Bluewater shopping centre or picture of a local town centre or shopping mall.

a purpose and a challenge

To reflect on the desire for material things, and on our enjoyment of leisure activities. How far do we want our religious activities to be attractive, entertaining and tailored to our own preferences?

some wider questions for discussion

● As Christians in mission, how important is it that we understand our own involvement in the shopping, leisure and entertainment cultures?

● Do you enjoy Christmas shopping? What have your experiences of Christmas shopping been like? How does Christmas shopping relate to church activities at Christmas?

● Do you prefer local shops and activities in the community or special trips out? Would people make a special trip to visit your church? What would you do to welcome them?

suggested passages for Bible study

Ecclesiastes 2.1-8
Matthew 6.19-24
Luke 18.18-27

meditation or music

Lord of the worlds above,
  how pleasant and how fair
the dwellings of thy love,
  thy earthly temples, are!
To thine abode
  my heart aspires,
  with warm desires
  to see my God.[3]

Isaac Watts

some thoughts about mission

How do we engage in mission towards those whose lives are
conditioned by our consumerist society? How do we help people to
think about their wealth and their options for saving or spending?
Are religious activities just another leisure activity? How far do we
spend time thinking about *stewardship* in the context of mission?

further resources

Michael Moynagh, *Changing World, Changing Church*, Monarch, 2001.
Mission Theological Advisory Group, *The Search for Faith and the
Witness of the Church*, Church House Publishing, 1996.
Jeanne Hinton, *Changing Churches: Building Bridges in Local Mission*,
CTBI, 2001.
Film: *American Beauty*, (Dreamworks LLC, 1999, directed by Sam
Mendes, produced by Bruce Cohen and Dan Jinks).

chapter 10

transformation

For a lighthearted meditation at Christmas, we used an excerpt
from *The Muppets' Christmas Carol*[1] to think seriously about what
Christmas means to people

prayer

Searching God,
you know the secrets of all our hearts.
Your Spirit comes to set us free.
Challenge and change us by your love
so that we may witness to you in the world.
Amen.

54

theological reflection

'Scrooge's song'

With a thankful heart, with an endless joy
with a growing family every girl and boy
will be nephew and niece to me,
will bring love hope and peace to me.
Yes and every night will end
and every day will start
with a grateful prayer and a thankful heart.

With an open smile and with open doors
I will bid you welcome, what is mine is yours,
with a glass raised to toast your health
and a promise to share the wealth
I will sail a friendly course
and file a friendly chart
on a sea of love and a thankful heart.

Life is like a journey, who knows when it ends?
Yes and if you need to know
the measure of a man
you simply count his friends.
Stop and look around you,
the glory that you see
is born again each day
don't let it slip away
how precious life can be.

With a thankful heart that is wide awake
I do make this promise: every breath I take
will be used now to sing your praise
and to beg you to share my days
with a loving guarantee that even if we part
I will hold you close in a thankful heart.

This song is sung by the actor Michael Caine as Ebenezer Scrooge
in *The Muppets' Christmas Carol*. Following the original by Charles
Dickens, the story concerns the conversion of the miserly Ebenezer
Scrooge to a kind, generous person who shows compassion for the
poor and for those in his employ. The Muppets version tells the story
with typical Muppet humour and it is easy to see the zany dialogue,
jokes and cute, cuddly animal figures as a schmaltzy version of a
well-worn morality tale.

Yet perhaps we should not dismiss a film like *The Muppets' Christmas Carol* as just children's entertainment. Scrooge's song has nothing explicitly Christian about it, and yet it echoes Christian sentiments. To begin and end each day with prayer and thanksgiving should be at the heart of our spiritual lives.

In the research by Professor David Hay and Dr Kate Hunt on *The Spirituality of People who don't go to Church*,[2] the authors note that Christmas still has a powerful hold on many people for whom Church is otherwise alien. This seems to be because there remains a powerful sense of nostalgia surrounding the events of Christmas and a strong memory of a time when all seemed to be well. *The Muppets' Christmas Carol* sums up some of these feelings. The original Dickens story may now have the trappings of easy entertainment, but at its heart the story of how a person's life can be changed still remains. There is no explicit reference to Jesus, except when Kermit remarks that the disabled Tiny Tim wanted others to remember who made the lame walk and the blind see. While we may feel that the sting of the social message has been watered down to give it a warm glow, nonetheless, at the very end of the film it is suggested that those people who enjoyed watching it should read the book! In the same way, perhaps the nostalgic memories surrounding the events of the Nativity could be used as a bridge back to the originating story in the Bible and to the centuries of Christian witness surrounding it.

some thoughts from the group

The Christian story has a powerful resonance, even for people well outside the Christian religion. There are also intimations of this in the Christmas celebrations, such as the symbols on Christmas cards and, in the television listings there is sometimes a whole string of programmes designed to evoke powerful emotions. We were aware of people who spent all year preparing for Christmas and who were tremendously excited by its possibilities and hopefulness when it arrived, only to be disappointed when other members of the family did not make the occasion as wonderful as they had hoped. We thought we could see this also in pop music where there is romantic idealization of the idea that 'all you need is love'. But the further question for us as Christians is: what does it demand of us to give and receive this love? We need to ask ourselves what happens when people regard the Christmas story as a romantic illusion. So how can we make the story become reality for people? What happens when people believe that our Christian faith is a lovely fantasy? The challenge is that there is a reality within our beliefs that goes well beyond illusions; for example one of the things that most moves us, within the content of the Christian story, is the idea of unconditional love and being loved for who we are. The difficulty is that sometimes words like 'love' lose their powerful content. Such words can be used all too easily.

We felt that memory was all important. The Prophets had continually articulated the message of God, lest people forget God in the time of their exile. For many, the Eucharist is a powerful evocation of important memory and Jesus said that we should do this specifically in memory of him. For this reason, we should not dismiss Scrooge's song out of hand if it reaches out to where people are. In Charles Wesley's hymns there was emotion coupled with content. For example, when Wesley was preaching outdoors, near Bristol, some people sang 'Nancy Dawkins' to upset him. He took the song and put new words to it. This brought tears to sailors' eyes, and resulted in many conversions. This all took place outside in the street. So, what makes for transformation and what content makes the difference? If all this can take place outside the institution, then how do we own it or recognize it, or do we merely want to cut it off, or even to take it over?

Yet there may be other, hostile, forces. For example, when Cliff Richard tried to release *The Lord's Prayer* there were efforts to keep it off pop radio. There was also a campaign of advertisements to stop people drinking and driving, which showed negative images of accidents against a background of traditional Christmas carols. This makes new kinds of connections in people's minds between what they hear and what they see. We need to share our faith, but also to be aware of other connections that are being made.

poems[3]

the kingdom of God
Our Father,
you are for turning;
turning us round
       upside down,
       inside out,
help us to give ourselves
to your revolution of
challenge and love,
through him who called for
turning and trust,
Jesus Christ our Lord,
Amen.

the strangeness of God
Our Father,
you are a wild God,
    yet we try to tame you;
you exiled your people,
     gave up your Son,
     raised up a convict,
     for our welcome home:
you are a free God,
yet we try to cage you.
Amen.

the foolishness of God
Our Father,
you are great and glorious;
but to this twisted world
your wisdom and power
seem stupid and feeble:
grant us your insight,
your subtlety and love,
to show you to people
as you really are,
focused in your Son,
Jesus Christ our Lord,
Amen.

Graham Kings

other paths for exploration

image or focus of meditation

Look at the image of Scrooge from a book illustration, or play the relevant section of *The Muppets' Christmas Carol*. What are your initial impressions?

a purpose and a challenge

Think about how the Holy Spirit changes minds and hearts. Do we make it possible for the Holy Spirit to work in others' hearts or do we get in the way?

some wider questions for discussion

● As Christians in mission, what do we think happens when people come to be converted to Christian faith?

- Can we share our own stories of coming to faith or conversion?
  What do people need from us to make changes in their lives?

- What other kinds of transformation would we wish to see in our
  own community?
  In what ways would it be possible for us to work towards change
  for the better?

suggested passages for Bible study

Luke 18.35-43
Acts 8.26-40
Acts 9.1-9

meditation or music

Love came down at Christmas,
    love all lovely, Love divine;
love was born at Christmas,
    star and angels gave the sign.[4]

               Christina Rossetti

some thoughts about mission

What does it take to bring about transformation in the world? How
can we bring back the emotional power and depth of John 3.16: 'God
so loved the world that he gave his only Son, so that everyone who
believes in him may not perish but may have eternal life'?

further resources

Charles Dickens, *A Christmas Carol* (1843), in *The Christmas Books*,
volume 1, Penguin, 1971.
Jostein Gaarder, *The Christmas Mystery*, Phoenix, 1996.
David Hay and Kate Hunt, *The Spirituality of People who don't
go to Church*, University of Nottingham, 2000. Available free via
www.ccom.org.uk, see downloads.
Janice Price, *Telling your Faith Story*, Church House Publishing, 1998.

notes

preface

1 Atkinson, David, *Jesus, Lamb of God*, SPCK, 1996.

chapter 1: vision

1 Published by HarperCollins (Flamingo), 1998.

2 Note that in Scripture Jared is the father of Enoch. See Genesis 3.13 and Luke 3.37.

3 Hymn 8 in *Hymns Ancient and Modern Revised*, William Clowes, 1950.

4 On the web site www.allmovie.com you can find lists of films with similar themes.

chapter 2: sacrifice

1 J. K. Rowling, *Harry Potter and the Philosopher's Stone*, Bloomsbury, 1997, p. 216.

2 These are all popular programmes aimed at teenagers and young adults, which have protagonists who interact with supernatural forces. *Buffy*, in particular, has a cult following as the 'vampire slayer', whose job is to protect the world from evil forces.

3 Richard Dawkins is the Charles Simonyi Professor of the Public Understanding of Science at Oxford University. He is the author of *The Selfish Gene* (1976), *The Extended Phenotype* (1986), *River out of Eden* (1995), *Climbing Mount Improbable* (1996), *Unweaving the Rainbow* (1998). He is well known for his view that religious belief distracts from a proper understanding of the world and our place in it.

4 *Gladiator*, directed by Ridley Scott, DreamWorks (USA)/Universal, 2000.

5 These words are spoken when Spock sacrifices himself in Star Trek II *The Wrath of Khan* (Paramount Pictures 1982, produced by Robert Sallin, directed by Nicholas Meyer). The words are reprised in Star Trek III, *The Search for Spock* (Paramount Pictures 1984, produced by Harve Bennett, directed by Leonard Nimoy) in which Spock returns from the dead. Captain Kirk is admonished by Spock's father, when Captain Kirk admits that he did not think about saving Spock's soul or his ultimate destiny.

6 From Hymn 67, *Hymns Ancient and Modern New Standard*, Hymns Ancient and Modern Ltd., 1983.

chapter 3: praise

1 Hymn 168, subtitled 'The glory and success of the Gospel' in *Hymns Ancient and Modern New Standard*, Hymns Ancient and Modern Ltd., 1983.

2 'God's Grandeur', in Gerard Manley Hopkins, *Poems and Prose*, selected and edited by W. H. Gardner, Penguin, 1953, p. 27.

3 This poem was first published in *Christian*, January 1990.

4   No. 336 in '100 Hymns for Today' in *Hymns Ancient and Modern New Standard*, Hymns Ancient and Modern Ltd., 1983.

5   'Praise You' is available on the album *You've come a long way, baby*, Skint Records, 1998. The video was created by the Torrance Community Dance Group. *Metro's* Keith Watson on 14 May 2002 commented 'Ingenuous to the point of heartbreak, the joy of movement has rarely been communicated more honestly', p. 17.

chapter 4: hope

1   This is a true story, but 'Corinna' is not her real name.

2   *The Gaze of Love*, p. 106.

3   Hymn 99 in *Hymns Ancient and Modern New Standard*, Hymns Ancient and Modern Ltd., 1983.

chapter 5: the cross

1   'The Dream of the Rood' in *Anglo-Saxon Poetry*, selected and translated by R. K. Gordon, Everyman's Library, Dent, 1976, p. 235.

2   An extended meditation on the sculpture by Jonathan Clarke written by the Revd Canon Dr Graham Kings is to be found in his lecture entitled 'Jesus Christ Saviour of the World' at www.martynmission.cam.ac.uk.

3   From the hymn 'Glorious things of thee are spoken' by John Newton (1725–1807) after Isaiah 33.20-21.

4   Origen (c185–c254) was a theologian born in Egypt and a student of Clement of Alexandria. One of his most important works is the *De Principiis*, a systematic theology dealing with God and God's relationship with the universe, the place of human beings, good and evil and the interpretation of Scripture.

5   Karl Rahner (1904–84) was a Jesuit theologian who taught at the universities of Innsbruck and Munich. An adviser to the Second Vatican Council, his thought is recorded particularly in his *Theological Investigations*.

6   Jonathan Clarke (born 1961) has contributed to the *Theology through the Arts* project of CARTS at Cambridge. He has also produced the Stations of the Cross and *Road to Emmaus* for Southwell Minster and *The Way of Life* for Ely Cathedral. All his works are unique, cast in aluminium using the lost polystyrene process.

7   Hymn 67, *Hymns Ancient and Modern New Standard*, Hymns Ancient and Modern Ltd., 1983.

8   Warner Brothers, 1986, produced by Fernando Ghia and David Puttman, directed by Roland Joffe. This film is about Father Gabriel, a priest who has come to spread the word of God among the Guarani Indians, and Rodrigo Mendoza, who has come to enslave them. The film is also especially noted for an extraordinary soundtrack by Ennio Morricone.

chapter 6: evil

1   Albert Camus, *The Plague*, translated from the French by Stuart Gilbert, Penguin, 1960, p. 178.

chapter 7: absence

1 R. S. Thomas, *Collected Poems*, Phoenix, 1995, p. 282.

chapter 8: loss

1 *The Catholic Prayerbook from Downside Abbey*, T&T Clark, 1999, p. 55.

chapter 9: desire

1 See www.bluewater.co.uk. The facts and figures in this section are taken from this web site.

2 Unlike Lakeside in Thurrock, where services are held by local clergy in a designated chapel.

3 Hymn 165 in *Hymns Ancient and Modern New Standard*, Hymns Ancient and Modern Ltd., 1983.

chapter 10: transformation

1 *The Muppets' Christmas Carol*, Columbia Pictures/Jim Henson Pictures, 1992, directed by Brian Henson.

2 *The Spirituality of People who don't go to Church*, University of Nottingham, August 2000. Available free via www.ccom.org.uk, see downloads.

3 These three poems were first published in the CMS Prayer Paper 1987.

4 Hymn 59 in *Common Praise*, Canterbury Press, 2000.

related titles from the Mission Theological Advisory Group

Presence and Prophecy
A heart for mission in theological education

This thoughtful and stimulating report asks what kind of teaching and learning experiences can help Christians to become people with hearts for mission. It takes a fresh look at elements of the theological curriculum and suggests a new vision and hope for all the Churches. *Presence and Prophecy* is ideal for anyone involved in theological education, whether in formal training for lay and ordained ministry or in other aspects of theological study.

£11.95 0 7151 5548 2

Presence and Prophecy Study Guide
A heart for mission in theological education

This study guide aims to help a variety of groups, including local churches, tackle the issues raised in *Presence and Prophecy*. It sets out ways of engaging with the ideas in the book, linking the themes and joining in an important conversation about how the Churches in mission can make a difference in people's lives.

£3.95 0 7151 5549 0